A Memoir

Finally
FREE

STEPHANIE
McKITTRICK

Finally
FREE

FINALLY FREE by Stephanie McKittrick
Published by stephaniemckittrick.com

Unless otherwise noted, all Scripture quotations are taken from the New King James Version®. Copyright © 1982 by Thomas Nelson. Used by permission. All rights reserved.

Scripture quotations marked ESV are from the Holy Bible, English Standard Version. Copyright © 2001 by Crossway Bibles, a division of Good News Publishers. Used by permission.

Visit the author's website at stephaniemckittrick.com.

International Standard Book Number: 978-1-7338730-9-3
E-book ISBN: 978-1-7352282-0-4

While the author has made every effort to provide accurate internet addresses at the time of publication, neither the publisher nor the author assumes any responsibility for errors or for changes that occur after publication. Further, the publisher does not have any control over and does not assume any responsibility for author or third-party websites or their content.

20 21 22 23 24 — 987654321
Printed in the United States of America

CONTENTS

Chapter 1

LIFE IS NO MOVIE

HAVE YOU EVER FELT LIKE YOUR LIFE was one big drama that moved from disaster to disaster? That's pretty much how my life was. Such is the life of an abused child. I grew up in Belfast, Northern Ireland, a church kid and the daughter of an abusive alcoholic father. When my dad got drunk, he would beat us, call us names, and scream at us for "making him bad." Then my ministry-trained father (who we called John) would go out and tell people about the love of Jesus. It was just us he hated.

Growing up in Belfast presented challenges of its own. From 1968 to 1998 we had what is known as "The Troubles" in Northern Ireland. This was a bitter civil war between Protestants and Catholics. Many people died during this war, many soldiers died and many atrocities were committed. Even to this day there are families grieving for sons and daughters that were murdered but their bodies have never been found. When you travel to another country and you talk about the time the IRA bombed your street and part of the roof of your house came off, that you realize just how different it is. Or you recall the time a car bomb went off down the street killing an innocent mother. It's hard to explain Belfast to people who have not lived here. I grew up with police checks on buses, seeing armed police walking around and used to seeing people rioting. It was "exciting" when you would see the army bringing in the huge water cannons to dispel the rioters. I remember one year when the rioter's hijacked a Dunkin Donut lorry. Looking out my bedroom window onto the main road out of town, I watched as the looters boarded the back of the lorry to recover the sugary load. The looters then set fire to the lorry and sold the donuts around the housing estate. We were all eating donuts for days. This was Belfast. Although life was tough in Northern Ireland, it was really all I ever knew.

My home life was far from the perfect picture of families portrayed on television. School wasn't much better; I was bullied and didn't have many friends. There was no escape from my cold reality of constant fear, shame, addiction, and poverty. I felt worthless twenty-four hours a day, seven days a week.

My mum was the only breadwinner in the family. She worked hard looking after elderly people all day and then in the evenings had an alcoholic husband to deal with. Life was really hard for her as well. She would work and my dad would drink her money. He would run up debts and she would have to work extra jobs to pay them. I remember one time she had four jobs at the same time. Home life was just manic. There was no peace, no joy, and no time for love. It was a journey of existence that we went on together.

The thing about being abused as a child is you begin to withdraw to make yourself invisible. Inside, you want to be loved and accepted like the other children but you also know that you have to protect yourself and the best way to do that is by not existing. Or at least appearing not to exist. At a very young age, I learned to put up walls and take a step back to protect myself by becoming invisible. It was better to hide away in a room or a corner somewhere than to be anywhere near my dad. If I needed a drink or snack, I waited until he was nowhere near the kitchen and then made my move, creeping along the hall and into the kitchen trying not to make any noise. I learned that the less he saw me, the less I got beat or screamed at.

As an abused child, you learn not to trust quiet and peaceful moments. You're constantly bracing yourself for the danger and chaos that is sure to come.

On one particularly terrifying occasion, my younger sister and I were at home playing together. Mum was at work, which meant no protection from John. Suddenly he started shouting at us and we knew what was coming. Panic set in. My dad grabbed my sister by the hair and pulled her out of the living room. I really thought he was going to do serious damage this time and my sister was going to end up in the hospital. I had to do something. My first instinct as a big sister was to defend her, so I jumped in between the two of them. In a rage, my dad delivered an almighty slap to my face with all of his strength that lifted my body off the ground and slammed me against the wall. Lying on the floor with pain shooting through my back, I began to hyperventilate; I was having an asthma attack. Struggling to breathe, I frantically searched my pockets, only to realize my inhalers weren't there. John moved around the house like a mad man. We didn't even know why he was angry. This was a whole new level. I lay on the ground trying to breathe, as my father, the man who was supposed to love and protect me, screamed at me and kicked me on the floor. My sister screamed for help desperately hoping someone would rescue us this time. She scrambled round the room to find my inhalers. When she found them, she ran as fast as she could to put them into my mouth. I took some puffs of my inhaler and slowly began to breathe again.

My sister saved my life that day. Our father didn't care.

After this near-death experience, I knew I had to take matters into my own hands. I had to find a place for my sister and me to live, where we would be wanted and loved. It was obvious: I needed to run away. I woke up in the middle of the night, dressed myself in my pink Barbie jeans and t-shirt, put on my trainers and packed a small bag with toys I could trade with people for money and I left home. I imagined that I could just leave that place and, just like in the movies, I would be taken in by a sweet stranger and have an adventure. In my head I was planning that once I got settled with my new family, I would go back and get my sister. At 6:00 a.m. I set off down the main road. It was a cold morning. I can remember the frost on the ground. I wasn't afraid. I felt free and even excited.

As I walked down my road, I figured it was a good idea to catch the bus into town; after all, Belfast City Centre was the center of the universe to an eight-year-old. Standing at the bus stop, I realized all the money I had in the world was literally just enough to pay my bus fare. I stood waiting. As the bus pulled up, I stepped on. Amazingly, the driver let me get on the bus on my own, no questions asked. Gazing out the window of the bus, I was already dreaming of the adventures and the new life I was about to have.

I had left behind the beatings, the hatred, and all the badness. Now, I was ready to live my life like the kids I saw on TV.

The bus stopped in Belfast City Centre and I got off. I had no idea where to go or what to do. I thought of all the shows I watched with friendly homeless people or bird ladies. I started walking to see if I could find any. As I walked through the streets, I noticed people looking at me. I wondered what they must have thought of an eight-year-old carrying a small backpack and a teddy bear, walking the streets alone. I stopped to look into the windows of one of the shops I had been to with my mother. As I looked at mine and my teddy bear's reflection in the window, I thought of all the times my mum had held my hand. I thought of how my sister laughed. What had I done? Was running away the right thing to do?

"Hey, you down there." I looked up and there at the top of a huge set of ladders was a window cleaner. "What are you doing out here on your own? It's dangerous. Where is your mummy?" I didn't want to say I was a runaway, but I hoped he would help me.

"You can't walk around here. I'm going to have to take you to the police station for them to get you home". I had a mixture of emotions. I so desperately wanted a new home. I didn't want my adventure to end here but I was also afraid. Running away wasn't as easy as it was in the films. Yes, going home meant I was returning to beatings and abuse but at least I would have my mum and my sister. The window cleaner took me by the hand and walked me to the nearest police station. One million thoughts were going around in my head. Would they jail me for running away? What would my father do when he saw me? Would my mum be angry? We arrived at the police station. I had never been in one before. It was so big; I could smell the cleaning agents on the floor.

There was a big window above my head and a policeman stood behind. He had on a blue uniform and he smiled at me. I sat down and watched as the window cleaner explained that I was a runaway and he had found me wandering through the town. I was nervous and embarrassed. Dad was always shouting that we could never get anything right and here, I couldn't even get running away right. I didn't want anyone to look at me. I just wanted to disappear. I fell asleep on the seats in the waiting room. When I woke up, my mum, dad and sister were standing there. They had come for me. Surely now my dad would realize how serious things were. Surely, he would start to be a father to us. Now, we could be a family. Maybe, just maybe I had managed to make him see how much he was hurting us. Maybe my adventure had been a success after all!

We got home and walked into our house. I sat on the sofa I had been beat on so many times. My mum asked, "Why did you do that? Why did you run away?" My dad started screaming at me. He screamed about how much money he had wasted going to get me. Nothing had changed. My eight-year-old heart sank again. This was my life. I was going to have to accept it. Maybe one day someone would notice a bruise on my face. Maybe someone would hear our screams and save us. Maybe my sister and I would be lucky enough to end up in the hospital and then they would take us away. This was my survival plan.

In this moment, I learned to accept abuse as a normality of my life. Right then, I accepted that I wasn't like other kids that can be loved and hugged. I knew I just had to get through life as quietly as I could and accept that I was always going to be on the bottom of the pile.

It is strange to look back on this now. I could never have known then, just how much this would impact the whole trajectory of my life—but it did. It really did. At that young age, I had accepted defeat. I learned that I wasn't as valuable as other kids. This acceptance of inferiority was my protection. It was my survival kit. As long as I didn't fight to be like anyone else, I could accept the abuse and just get through the days. I reasoned that eventually I would die, and it would all be over.

I am the typical child abuse story: Abused at home, bullied in school, no friends, living with shame and poverty, falling in with the bad crowd, turning to alcohol and drugs by thirteen. How many more people out there have a similar story? Why are so many stories the same? How is it that so many can go through all the bad stuff and the only comfort they can find is in drugs?

It just seemed that no matter what I did or how hard I tried, I messed up. I messed up everything. It was always my fault. That's just how it was. If something went wrong around me, I was conditioned to take the blame and the punishment, even if I had nothing to do with it.

My mum kicked my dad out of the house when I was thirteen, but the damage had already been done. I was on a path to nowhere. Any notion or dreams of success for the future had been slapped out of me. All I wanted was someone to love and accept me, but I was convinced that people saw me as poor, dirty, unlovable, and beneath them. I could see it when they looked at me, they knew I was beneath them, I was less than them. I knew people could see that I was poor, dirty, and unlovable. I searched for a place where I could at least sit in; because I knew I would never fit in. I looked for someone who could handle my tenuous or fragile existence and never-ending drama.

Across from our house lived a girl who was a couple of years older than I was. Her name was Natalie. She seemed popular and a bit crazy, but she was nice. I couldn't believe she wanted to be my friend. Finally, someone was interested in me.

"You can come hang out with us," she said. "There is a whole big group of us in this estate. I will look after you."

She promised everything I wanted, hoped for, and prayed for. She promised friendship, an escape from my house, somewhere I could just be with other people and be a part of life. For so many years now, I had been trying to hide, to be invisible but I wanted to LIVE, to be a part of something. I wanted friends and to be popular. I wanted to be wanted and to feel accepted.

"Do you smoke? Have you any fags on you?"

I started smoking in school but clearly not as much as she did. There was something different about her, I couldn't figure it out. Everyone seemed to be afraid of her, but she was so nice to me. She was the only one that was nice to me. I had found my place.

This new relationship came with a lot of new friends. For the first time I had people who wanted me around, even if it was only to use me. At that time in my life I was desperate for acceptance and love that I was prepared to do whatever it took to fit in.

At night, I waited until my mum was sleeping and crawled out the living room window to go meet my new friends. What a buzz. Creeping out of my bedroom in the middle of the night with my stomach churning knots, I felt so free. I felt as if nothing could stop me. Our living room window was large, and it unhinged in a way so I could fit right through it. Once I got through the window, I closed it and tiptoed out the driveway making sure no one in the house could hear me. My new friends stood at the end of the driveway and laughed as I ran up the path. This was my new life of adventure. Wasn't this a part of growing up? I was having fun and my mum knew nothing about it, so she couldn't ruin it for me.

My friends always hung out with older

guys who had cars. I never understood how they knew so many guys, but they did, and I was just happy to be a part of it. I loved when we would go out in the cars and drive fast through the country backroads. The music was always too loud to hear people talking and I preferred it that way. I could feel the vibration of the music throughout my body and escape into a place in my imagination where I was living a different life. There were no streetlights on those country backroads and all you could see was the couple of feet in front with the car lights. I loved it! I enjoyed the danger and the thrill of not knowing what was around the next corner. These wild and crazy adventures of racing around in the dark with little to no light echoed my life. I was getting a taste of what it felt like to live life on my terms and doing whatever I wanted, whenever I wanted.

As my circle of "friends" grew, I increasingly found myself involved in fights or arguments with other kids. This was a whole new ball game to me. I was not naturally a fighter and because I grew up with an abusive father, I would have never dreamed of hurting someone. But with this reckless lifestyle came a boldness I had not known before. I was in situations where I had to stand my ground and learn to defend myself. I chose to live a life without fear! I decided that nothing would scare me, and I would push back at anyone who tried to intimidate me. After all, if I was able to withstand beatings from a grown man, there wasn't much any teenager could do to really hurt me.

It was a dangerous mindset, but it was my reality. In a twisted way, it was empowering to think that my ability to endure years of abuse and chronic asthma made me unstoppable. It was like I had this secret power no one knew about.

Throughout my childhood and teenage years, I was always sick. I had almost died many times. I would joke to cover up my fear and the effects of all my pain and suffering, but it was all a lie. Deep down, I knew my life sucked. I wasn't unstoppable: I was self-destructive.

Natalie was a couple of years older than me and was already going to nightclubs and she was more than happy to get me in as well.

The first nightclub I went to was called "Paradise Lost", it was dark, and it was "rough". When you walked in there was a wooden bridge that you crossed over into the club. The dance floor was deep in the floor, very much like a pit and there were statues around of angels and demonic heads. Of course at the time I never thought anything about this, I was just lost in the excitement of being in a nightclub at the grand old age of 14 but now, knowing what I know…my goodness. Paradise Lost is a poem written by a 17th Century poet, John Milton. His poem tells the epic biblical story of the fall of man, the temptation of Adam and Eve by the fallen angel, Satan and their expulsion from the Garden of Eden. I was certainly no angel but this was definitely a place of falling for me. Here I got my first introduction to Class A drugs. I loved being there, the music literally pumping through your body, standing on the dance floor "completely off my face" on a cocktail of drugs. This was a world away from my reality. Here I wasn't someone to be screamed at and yelled at. Here I wasn't

an abused kid. Here, I was just like everyone else.

I tried to be the good girl by going to
college and staying away from anyone that
drank or took drugs, but it never lasted long.
I loved the feeling of being on ecstasy tablets and I loved the feeling of snorting a line
of cocaine. How it rushed up your nose, hit
your brain and gave you that "ahh…" feeling. I loved going to nightclubs knowing I
was underage. It was the thrill. I had tasted
danger and there was no turning back.

It took me a few years of practice to find
something I was good at, which, as it turned
out, was getting unbelievably wasted. I could
drink and take more drugs than anyone else
I knew. I share all of this because I know
there are so many women out there like me
who are hurting and trying to make sense of
their lives. I was a complete mess.

I accepted this was my reality. This was
my life and it was the best someone like me
could hope for. Even in my own eyes I would
never be respected or valued. This was my
life and I just had to accept that. Except, I
now know that is a lie and if I can help just

one person realize that they can get out of the pit, then this was worth it. If you have a pulse, which I am assuming you do if you are reading this, then that pulse is confirmation that you have a hope and a future. Later on, in the book, we will talk about how you get there.

Stuff happened to me in my childhood that wasn't my fault but impacted my whole life. It shaped me. It shaped my thinking and pushed me into a destructive path. I dedicated myself to walking blindly on this dark path, blind to the truth.

As years went by, my life was a complete blur. I went from one circle of people to the next, but I could not find my place. I was never really into relationships. I knew more drug dealers than people who I could actually call friends. I just wanted to have a good time. Years of dysfunction crafted a fragmented young adult whose greatest achievement was being able to swallow eight ecstasy pills in one go. I was known by everyone as the girl who was the life and soul of the party. I laughed the most and the loudest, but I was broken. I had lost all hope for a good life and accepted a lesser standard of partying and drugs. This is the life I had chosen. I wasn't hurting anyone else but myself.

People look at me now and think I have it all together, not knowing that I was once broken, abused, and abandoned. I was the same as any other addict sitting on the street corner. The only difference was I had a post code and a bed to sleep in at night.

It's very easy to judge someone who is in the pit when you don't know the path that led them there. Solutions seem simple for someone who is observing the drug addict on the street corner as they can walk out of their office in their nice suit on their way to a lovely home. They may look at what seems like a wasted life and assume that the obvious answer would be for that person to stop taking drugs without considering all of the hurt and circumstances that contributed to the addiction. Sometimes the reality of life is so heavy that instead of trying to carry it, you just let go and let it carry you.

Chapter 2

COCAINE, COCKTAILS, AND MAKING BABIES

A S YOU CAN SEE, WHEN I WAS A MESS, a lot of people around me thought I was just "mad"—a fun, outgoing, party girl. I bet if you spoke to some of those people today, they will have a hard time accepting what I am saying to you now, because I lived under a mask I created as a child to protect myself. This mask became my identity.

Now don't get me wrong, I had a lot of great nights out. I loved nothing more to get wasted, but truthfully, I was just hiding from my own reality. I was the loudest in any room, always had jokes and was up to something funny, but I was shielding deep wounds—wounds that ran so deep, they came from my soul.

It's funny because often at parties, the subject would turn to religion. Living here in Northern Ireland where we were still heal-ing from "the Troubles," a bitter religious civil war, it wasn't hard for us to start talking about our faith, whatever amount we had. In these conversations I always said I believed in God, even though I had no experience of Him. Something, somewhere deep inside of me had a hope that He was real. It was a nice thought to believe there was a God, but I was so alone all the time.

Loneliness is difficult to deal with. From being a child, hiding in the halls from my abusive father to having no friends in school, my playground had just changed shape. One thing I learned is that there is no amount of cocaine, cocktails, or anything else that can fill that void. Trust me, I tried.

Sure, you can escape for a few hours, but when you are home alone and the come-down hits, so does reality. The feelings of emptiness create an echo for a desperate inner cry for more, all while you are trapped by circumstance. Putting on a show and getting through the days is how I lived my days. I could feel my mask slipping; I needed to take control of my life. I needed to up my game. I needed to do something.

I wanted to be one of those women with the nice house in a nice area with a garden, husband and 2.4 children. What made them so different from me? Why was it that I was such a mess? Why did I repel everyone around me? Leveling up was going to take a miracle for me and one thing was sure: I needed to stop partying almost every night.

So, with my big-girl pants on and a straight head, I enrolled to study accountancy at night in college, the obvious progression for my current job and I was determined. During the day, I worked for a utilities company in Finance. Things started to look up, and I was winning at work, being given more responsibilities, and I was stepping up to the plate. Finally, I was lifting my head a little.

One particular month, I had set myself an incredibly high goal at work. When I shared it, everyone laughed at me, but I put my mind to it and achieved it. To celebrate, I went out with some work friends to a trendy bar in town straight after work. There was only one way that was going to end, and it was going to be messy.

Nights out after work, where that one drink you go for turns into thirty, always seemed to be the best! We spent a fortune on shots, shots, and more shots! Dancing, laughing, spilling drinks, laughing, smoking and laughing, it was a good time. One by one, people started to fade. Not me. I had staying power, and there was no way I was finishing my night at 2:00 a.m. on a Friday. So, I left with one of my work colleagues, Julienne, to go to her house.

Julienne was different, she had a family, a nice home, a good job, she had all the good stuff and was still partying. This is what I wanted. We just clicked. I wanted to grow up, settle down but I didn't want to give up my social life! I didn't want to give up partying, it was all I really knew.

Over the next few months, Julieann and I became great friends. Every weekend we hit her house, with one intention on our minds: to get as wasted as possible and drink away all our cares! As far as we could see, we worked hard during the week and deserved it. We had some great laughs. I was still studying accounting, although with each lesson, I hated it a little more and completely lost interest. Still, I kept going as I was paying for it.

Every party there would be between 6–10 of us there and when we got together, we were there for the weekend. Sleeping is cheating, you just keep drinking and snorting and you get through the weekend. Don't get me wrong, we had a lot of laughs, but the reality is, we were a group of adults, drinking and dancing in an outbuilding. Hanging up on the walls where various DIY tools and "handy" things for the house. Things I had never thought of owning. But we didn't care, we had a place that we could be in, where no-one saw us, and we could play music. We even had some mini fridges where we could store our drinks to keep them cold, we weren't complete savages (ha). This was just a new group of friends I had, that were settled in life, no drama, no fighting and they accepted me, but the conversation always had the same theme, why was I still single? Why I was not hitched?

One Halloween, we were gearing up for an outstanding night and Julieann kept telling me about this guy, Billy. Apparently, he was a great guy and I just had to meet him. Cue eyeball rolling from me.

This is where I am going to have to fast forward a bit. Things started off great. He really made me laugh, went out of his way to take me out for dinner and when I got home from college at night after work, he had a hot bath and a meal waiting on me. I was really happy. I thought I had arrived at my happy ending. Boy was I wrong. All my life I just wanted to be like other people. I was constantly trying to fit in with this group of people and that group of people. I could never just be me. Here was a guy who appeared to love me for me. I was completely blinded by my perception of what love was. My perception of love was someone that could be around you every day without screaming at you, starting fights with you and actually wanted to be in your company. That for me was love. When you have little to no self-worth, you will accept behavior that most would not. I was failing forward. Moving through life, going from one disaster to the next, hoping to catch a break somewhere. A break that never seemed to come.

For the next chapter of my life, all I can say is this: Ladies, if you ever find yourself in a relationship where he likes to control, play mind games, and mess you around, run. Run as fast as you can. You deserve so much better, and trust me, having no one is better than someone who wants to dangle you on a string.

All my life, things fell apart, and now I was admitting defeat again! Suddenly, the cracks began to appear. He was checking my phone all the time, he blocked me off all his social media accounts and was constantly asking where I was. But...I thought this was just a part of life. I had heard so many other stories of women complaining about a partner checking in on them all the time so I just figured, this was normal and that I was better getting on with things instead of causing a fuss. Years of abuse as a child taught me to be quiet and just keep going. It was good training for this. Even though he was not physically abusive, the mental torture was worse. Bruises on the skin fade but ones on the inside are a lot harder to heal. I couldn't give up, I was so close to being happy and having a normal life. I was just going to put up with whatever I could and just get through because I honestly didn't think I would ever get any better. I was so terrified of a lifetime alone that I was willing to put up with being treated like an animal.

Please learn from my mistakes, learn from my pain. I was willing to be ignored in my own home. I was willing to stay at home 24/7 with no life of my own. I was willing to do whatever it took to just not be alone. When you are in the pit, it's hard to see a way out, especially when there are no ladders. I know that I recoiled into myself in a way of trying to make the best of things until someone rescued me. But who? No one was even aware of what was going on at home. No one was going to rescue me because I hadn't screamed for help. No one was going to rescue me because I hadn't even fully realized the danger I was in. I had been conditioned my whole life to live in someone else's shadow, so this, was just a different shade of my abusive normal. This was just a different shade of life. But I knew deep down, I had to get away. Deep down, I knew there was more to life. If you are in that place get away from a guy like this, do it as fast as you can.

Through this relationship is how I have my beautiful daughter Lexie, my goodness. I was so blessed when I had her. She made everything in my life seem right. She made everything in my life have a purpose. By giving birth to her, I had a reason to live. I loved being her mummy and looking after her. It was going to be me and her against the world.

Billy was around from time to time but never consistently. It really was just Lexie and me, and I loved it. I was going to do whatever it took to be the best mummy I could be and my little girl would never have the childhood I had.

So, I was in this house; it was rented. I had nothing, literally nothing, not even a spoon! Thankfully some friends gave me some things. Every penny I got, I knuckled down, hustled, and I managed to make a home for my princess—a little girl who would become my best friend, who would grow up knowing she was loved, and who wouldn't grow up in fear. No matter what, she would never be in a place where she feels less than worthy. I didn't know how. I just knew I was going to make her proud.

Then when Lexie was about eleven months old, I started feeling sick again. Morning sickness is awful. I couldn't believe this feeling was rising up in me again. No way. I was seriously terrified now! How could I raise two kids alone?

I was pregnant and single. I had Lexie and now I was pregnant again. Sure, it was exciting that Lexie would have a brother or sister but how would I look after two children alone? How could I afford two children? Bill was already saying that he was not going to pay towards any children. He enjoyed the power he felt he had over me. He knew I was afraid and that he could control me by threatening to disappear out of our lives. He would text me gloating that he would never pay for any kids and he loved every second of it. He had already ditched me once. What would happen now? Immediately the panic button in my head was screaming. I had one million reasons this was awful but the one thing that defeated them all, was I knew how much I loved Lexie and I would love this baby, too.

As the days went on, oh my goodness, I

was so tired. I was determined to be the best mum I could be but literally this pregnancy was killing me! Oh, how little did I know. My morning sickness was horrendous, and I literally was gushing liquid 24/7 (sorry, but you need to get an idea). This was constant water, bile and vomit coming out of my mouth. I couldn't eat and I could barely drink. It got to the point I was vomiting so much that all I could manage to eat was a handful of jelly sweets and that was purely to try and take some of the acidic taste out of my bile. Life was grim. My head was in agony every day and I was so dizzy. As I pushed Lexie to the shops in her pram, my balance was off and I looked drunk. However, true to form, I kept going.

I was really struggling with Lexie on my own and this pregnancy. It became clear there was something much more than pregnancy sickness. I could barely stand and if I even looked a fraction in a different direction, I fell over. I was a complete mess.

Then one morning my life changed forever.

I went along for the twenty-week scan!

Exciting times usually! I was looking forward to finding out if I was having a boy or a girl. I was full of excitement; the sun was shining.

As I was sitting on the bed with the nurse scanning me, she went very quiet, which made me nervous, and I talk too much when I am nervous. It's a dangerous combo. She then suddenly said, "What's that!"

I nervously said, "What's what?"

Awkward silence.

Then there was a procession of fetal medical doctors, midwives, nurses, lots of people coming in to deliver the news. They told me my baby girl had CDH (congenital diaphragmatic hernia) and she had the rarer form of it and had a 20–30 percent survival rate.

I honestly felt like I had been stunned. I was in shock. I couldn't really take it in. I thanked them for their time and went home. I needed time to process what I had just heard. I just wasn't expecting it. I didn't want this to happen. None of this was part of the plan.

As soon as I got home I did the worse thing possible, I started googling and of course saw every worst case scenario on the net. I was so upset.

That night I fell asleep before my head hit the pillow because of the exhaustion of crying so much. Morning came. I woke, but I didn't get up. I just opened my eyes, and it literally felt as if the world collapsed. I can't really describe it but it was the most sickening, sinking feeling ever and I fell off the bed onto the floor. I couldn't see. Everything was spinning. I cried out and reached out and could feel the wall. I started vomiting so violently. Lexie was crying in her cot. I needed to get to her.

I crawled on my hands and knees into Lexie's cot and I lay on the floor beside her. I had my sick bowl with me. I tried to distract her while this awful spinning was happening. My legs just wouldn't work properly. I had no idea what was going on. I was desperately ill.

Somehow, I managed to crawl downstairs on my bum, taking one step at a time, and I got my phone and rang my mum. As soon as she heard my condition, she said straight away that she would take me to the emergency department at the hospital. At this stage we had been up there weekly if not daily because my sickness was so severe.

After what seemed like hundreds of trips to the Accident and Emergency (A&E) room at the hospital and never getting anywhere, my mum couldn't take it anymore. Every day we thought my baby and I would die and no one was helping us. I was in so much pain, vomiting nonstop, unable to walk properly or stand. Mum, in desperation, cornered one of the nurses and said, "If she was carrying a healthy child, you would have her looked at instead of leaving her like that! I'm telling you, if either of them die, I'm holding you responsible!" A mother's got to do what a mother's got to do sometimes.

This was enough to spur the nurse into action and before I knew it, a neurological consultant came to see me. She assessed me and agreed, it was definitely a lot more than morning sickness and I needed immediate hospitalization and scanning. I was so relieved. Finally, someone was actually going to do something to help.

What was happening to me? All I wanted

was to be a mum to my girls and raise them as best as I could. I had never killed anyone. I had never been really bad. I just wanted to love my girls. Here I am a single mother pregnant with a dying baby and potentially dying myself. How is this happening? It's just not fair! It's really not! I haven't done anything to deserve any of this. I wanted it to stop. But this was only the beginning.

If you remember, I mentioned that my life went from disaster to disaster. Well, that's exactly how it was; I never seemed to have peace in my life. For 10 years of my life I was a party girl, but I made a committed effort to be a mother as soon as my daughter was born. There was no transition period and no gradual moving into the next phase. Nope, I was a crash, bang, wallop through life, kinda girl. Now I know it's because I was always striving through life, striving to survive but I had never found the lane I was supposed to be in. I can look back now and see that I was so blind to the world around me. Everyone else seemed to have well-grounded people around them, they knew how to function in the world. I didn't. I was the proverbial bumper car, stuck in a one-track way to no-where with plenty of knocks along the way. Why though? What was it about me that was so disastrous? Why could I not fit into the world? I was in the world, but I seemed to be so out of the world in the sense, I didn't fit anywhere. However, despite my failings and shortcomings, somehow I was going to figure this out. I desperately wanted to be a good mother, to love my children and give them a good life. I wanted to give them the life I never had. I wanted them to be healthy and well. I wanted to pour out love on them that I never had. I wanted them so much. I never expected motherhood to be *this* hard.

Chapter 3

THE DAY THAT
CHANGED EVERYTHING

IMAGINE WAKING UP EVERY DAY TO THE possibility of death. I continued to experience difficulty standing and I was vomiting nonstop. I worried about how I would keep myself and my unborn baby alive. On top of all that, I had a one year old child to look after. This was my daily truth and my nightmare.

People always say, "Stephanie, you are so strong!" I didn't see myself as strong; I just did what I had to do to stay alive. I cried so much. I wanted the pain to stop. I frantically thought of everything possible to try and change my situation, but I could not get past the reality that no one was coming to save me. I screamed on the inside and sometimes outwardly. I don't know how many times I cried out to God and promised that if He would stop this pain I would be a good Christian and go to church. I was desperate.

In the midst of relentless pain I determined that my two girls and I would get through this. I began blocking out every negative thought. I knew that if I was going to survive this, I had to be my own biggest supporter. I had to push through. I was living in complete emotional and physical torment. All hell was breaking loose, but I had to focus on the task at hand: getting my baby full term.

On the day, I was admitted into the neurosurgery ward, I received a visit from the fetal medical team. They offered me a trip to London to medically terminate my baby. I had known women who had abortions. Whenever the issue came up in discussions, I always said, "Hey, their body, their choice." But this time was different. This time it was *my* baby, my body, my choice. I literally had to make a decision between life and death.

At that time abortion was all over the news and had just been legalized in Northern Ireland. I began researching abortions and how they were performed. In my heart, I could not reconcile terminating my pregnancy once I realized the truth. It is important for me to say that I would never judge anyone who has aborted a child because

I understand the pain, fear, and turmoil of facing that dilemma. After seeing what abortion does to unborn babies, I just couldn't do it. I wanted my baby to live even though I knew I would be risking my own life.

Abortion was not an option for me. They made the offer three times and each time I declined. I saw my babies as gifts, and it was my job to love them and cherish them. There was no way I was going to abort my baby to save my own life. Most mothers would die for their children and I was prepared to fight to the death for mine. Yes, I had Lexie to think of, but I heard something inside saying, "You *will* get through this. This is not how your story ends".

The medical team told my mum to prepare because I probably wouldn't make it. However, I knew different. This wasn't it. This wasn't the end of me.

To compound my suffering, during my stay in hospital, I underwent a surgical procedure in which holes were drilled into my skull and probes inserted that would attach to a laptop to measure the flow of my CSF or brain fluid. Patients are normally put to sleep to perform this procedure. However, because of my pregnancy, I was going to have to be awake. I was suffering that much; I was willing to do almost anything to get some relief. I developed intolerance to anti-sickness medication and couldn't have strong pain meds. It was torture.

When you are pregnant, your sense of smell is usually heightened and even the slightest unpleasant smell can make you vomit. Imagine me, already vomiting 300 times each day, in indescribable pain with my head and the "smell" of a neurosurgery ward. I've never been a fan of hospital food but all throughout the ward you could smell the steamed, stale scent of hospital food that I am not even sure can be legally called food. Mix that with the cleaning materials used to clean the wards and also taking into consideration the side effects of neuro meds on patients' bodily functions—gross! For a pregnant woman in my condition, the smell was just awful.

The nurses gave me a surgical gown and wheeled me into a treatment room. I was afraid to even look around in case I saw any of the surgical instruments. I didn't want to know what they were doing. I just wanted them to hurry up and get it done. I kept telling myself it was a short procedure and soon I would be back on the ward with my daughter, Lexie. This was just something I had to do. I had built myself for the process, but when the time came it was horrific.

I sat on the end of the bed, my pregnant belly poking through the hospital gown. I struggled to stay upright; I was dizzy, I almost fell off of the bed a couple of times, but nurses caught me. When they told me they were going to numb the skin on my skull, I was relieved. I was so tense. A large circular sheet was placed on top of my head. I couldn't see out of it. Then I heard a sound I will never forget; the drill being turned on. It was a million times worse than the dentist. The surgeon drilled three holes into my head. It really was awful. I sat under the sheet, crying, with both hands on my baby bump. I was doing this for her. Everything was for her. I felt a little trickle of blood escape through the sheet and it just mixed in with my tears. At this point, I realized that I really would do anything for my children.

The surgery was over in approximately forty minutes; the longest forty minutes of my life. I was given two paracetamol for pain and returned to the ward. I was so heartbroken. All my life I fought to be normal and here I was living like this. How could this be happening? Everyone talks about the goodness of God. How could He allow this? What kind of a God allows mothers to suffer like this? Even in my doubt and confusion I asked God not to take my baby and to keep me alive for Lexie.

"PLEASE GOD! HELP ME!" I cried out.

I was becoming a permanent feature on the neurosurgery ward, a place I dubbed "Death Row." Death Row was the bay for patients who needed urgent care. Two beds down from me was a man who had to be restrained in his bed because he had a massive brain injury and it affected his personality. If he didn't get his own way, he would defecate in the bed. The smell was horrendous to my pregnant nostrils.

Once I got up to go to the toilet. As

I walked past this man's bed, he started to pleasure himself. I was absolutely horrified.

I called for a nurse. "Nurse, that man is pleasuring himself while watching me", the nurse replied, "Oh Stephanie, I will pull his curtains around him. He doesn't know what he's doing; he had a serious head injury and has been confined to a bed for years. He is restrained so he can't get out to you".

This was too much. I just wanted to go home. I had enough to deal with never mind this. I pleaded with the nurses and doctors to let me go home and they agreed as they were unable to treat me due to my pregnancy.

I received an urgent telephone call from my neurosurgeon's secretary. They wanted to see me at the hospital. So mother and I went straight away. When I stepped into his office, I noticed it was just a treatment room with a desk in it. Strangely, there were no medical certifications on the wall. I wondered if he had another office that we weren't allowed access to. Maybe this was just a treatment room. However, I was expecting him to give me some hope, some encouraging news. After all, I was fighting for my life and the life of my unborn child. Surely that is something to be commended in the medical world.

The porter ushered me out of the wheelchair and onto the treatment bed. As I sat on the edge, I was clinging on the metal frame. My balance was so off I felt I would fall right off the bed. I was now at the stage I couldn't hold myself up without the room spinning at 360 mph. He told me, "Stephanie, you need emergency brain surgery and we cannot treat you because of this pregnancy. We have to tell you to make arrangements for your other daughter, Lexie, if the worst should happen which is most likely".

I had to keep pushing on. I had to keep my head straight. I had to keep thinking like a champion. I set my mind to see this like a race and we were running for our lives. I knew that if I could just get to the finish line we would all make it. It would be over and I could take my two girls home. I was fully prepared to take care of my baby if she had complications. She was mine and I would love her no matter what. I was determined to get to that finish line, even if I had to crawl my way there trailing a sick bucket behind me.

I felt trapped, but I wasn't beaten. No, I was far from it.

One night I sat in the bath crying with no lights on and overcome with every emotion you can imagine. Lexie was strapped into her bouncer beside the tub. I received a text from Penny, the wife of my mum's pastor. I had never even met her. In her text she wrote that a huge battle was raging for me in heaven and that I needed to commit my life to God.

I was furious. Imagine using my situation to try and get me into church. I got out of my bath in such a rage, rang my mum and gave her, as we say in Belfast, "dog's abuse." I would not tolerate her going around to churches telling people my business!

Thirty-six weeks into my pregnancy, I was called into a side room by the fetal specialist. "Stephanie, I have to prepare you. You are going to have to turn off her life support." I almost choked. What was this man talking about? Was he completely off his head? No! No, I wouldn't do it! My child would get out of this alive and no one or nothing could stop this. I had gotten us this far, only a few weeks left to go. I was so outraged that he would speak to me in such a manner. Obviously, I now know that he was doing the right thing but at the time, my heart and ears, just couldn't receive it. I was in full fight mode.

Two weeks later, after an awful day with the father of my children, I was at home feeling worthless. I cried myself to sleep that night. At 3:00 a.m. I awoke to find that my water had broken. I ran downstairs to tell Billy that it was time. We had to go! I rang my mum and stepdad. My stepdad watched Lexie while the rest of us went to the hospital.

The combination of contractions, neuro sickness, and car sickness was unbearable. Car journeys were the worst for me at this time. Even being pushed by a nurse in a wheelchair was too much motion for me, so you can use your imagination of what it was like with my mum flying through town in her car to get me to the hospital. Even in my discomfort, I was excited because I knew this was it. I knew I was getting my baby girl. I would have proved them all wrong.

We got to the hospital and I was admitted onto the labor ward. I laid in the bed struggling with the contractions and the sickness, but I was just so glad that I had made it this far.

I sat up overnight in my hospital bed, panicking. What if my baby came and the medical team wasn't prepared? What if the doctor hadn't reviewed the file and didn't understand how ill my daughter was? Why was no one taking control of the situation? Two lives were at risk here. I tried to quiet my mind, but my fears began to rise with every contraction.

The next day, before delivery I was given full anesthesia because an epidural would have killed me. When I woke up, the first words I spoke were, "Is she alive?".

I just wanted to see my baby. I wanted to meet her. I was moving in and out of consciousness, but I was still fighting. I knew I wanted to name her Layla. The nurses wanted me to wait a while before taking me to see her, but I was persistent. They agreed to wheel my whole bed up to see her.

Going into the fetal unit was daunting

because of all the tiny helpless babies in incubators. In the left corner of the unit was one baby surrounded by lots of machines. I just knew that was Layla. I had never seen anything like it. The machines were large and quite loud. The room was kept cold to keep the massive machines from overheating.

There she was, my beautiful baby girl. She was six pounds and three ounces of gorgeousness. She was here. Oh, my goodness. I loved her so much. My love saw past all the wires and machines. My heart literally ached to hold her, but all I could do was touch her tiny hand. I was desperately ill and required heavy duty pain meds. I was really doped up and still vomiting, but the nurse allowed me to stay.

I sat and looked at her and I begged God not to take my baby. God didn't need my baby, but I did.

The doctor came to me and said "Stephanie, we have to inform you that we have scanned Layla and she just does not have the organs capable for life or surgery. You have a choice here; you can turn off her life support and love her in the time you have or you can keep her going but the outcome will be the same."

I just wanted him to stop talking. This couldn't be the end. This isn't how it was supposed to be. I got us here. Inside I was screaming and trying not to fall apart. My baby looked so normal. You wouldn't have known by just looking at her that she was only being kept alive by machines. I was in this strange place of between shock and numbness. I couldn't wrap my head around what was happening. This is the kind of thing you read about in the papers, but it doesn't happen to you. But it was happening and I had a decision to make. So, I decided to have Layla baptized at 2:00 a.m. and removed from life support.

That night I wrestled with God in my bed and begged Him not to take my baby. I vowed to do anything, give anything, and be anything He wanted me to be if He would just please not take my Layla. Had I not suffered enough? Lexie needed her mum and her sister. "God, please," I pleaded.

Morning came.

My two best friends, Linda and Emma

came to visit me in the hospital. They pretended to be my sisters so that they could get onto the ward. Knowing my history of abandonment and that I was alone at the hospital, they came to offer their support. I wanted them to meet Layla before she was removed from the machines. My mum brought Lexie and my stepdad, Albert. It was time. This was really happening. No miracle had happened overnight.

We were taken into a special room for families that were spending the last moments with their baby. The nurses were fantastic. They knew how to take control and gave us advice of what pictures to take. I was still passing in and out of consciousness and throwing up. They agreed to increase my meds to help me get through the day.

I loved her so much. I tried not to love her too deeply because I knew I wouldn't be able to keep her. But oh, my goodness, I loved her. She was my beautiful girl. She was Lexie's sister. She was everything I was fighting for.

The hospital gave us a box filled with disposable cameras and different little items to help you remember the baby. This was just before smartphone technology. We took pictures of us all with her. We loved her as much as we could in the short amount of time that we had with her.

Every time we kissed her, she would open her wee eyes and look at us. I believe it was her way of letting us know she felt our love. I kept asking the nurses if she was in pain or suffering and they reassured me that she wasn't. One by one the machines were taken away until it was just us. She was so tiny wrapped up in a blanket. I was almost afraid to hold her because I didn't want to hurt her, but I also didn't want to let go. I tried to block off any feelings of hurt. I just needed to get through it. This was happening and I couldn't change it.

The time was close. The nurse came into the room and asked everyone to leave so I could have some time alone with Layla. What do you say in those moments? If I am brutally honest, I almost wanted it to end because I was so terrified of her suffering. I didn't want her to feel any pain. I was so aware that the machines were gone except the one for pain relief.

I sat with my baby and told her how much I loved her. I told her I was so sorry that I didn't find a way to help her stay.

A nurse came in to check her vitals again and said it was almost time to go. She walked away.

I looked at Layla, kissed her on the head and this time she didn't open her eyes. I knew she was gone. I called the nurse back and she confirmed. Layla had gone. It was over.

I took a deep breath and I just held it.

Having to hand your baby back is the hardest thing possible because you know that it's over and you have to let go.

I kept holding my breath and tried to block out all thoughts. As I was wheeled up to the special unit for mothers with sick and dying babies, I realized that I had only twenty-five hours with my daughter. I couldn't believe it. Just twenty-five hours with her. It wasn't fair.

I lay on the bed and I just burst into tears. A cry came out of the depths of my soul. This pain was far deeper than anything I had experienced before. I sat and I looked out of the window. Staring at the sky, I decided that there clearly wasn't a God. I also made a firm decision that I was going to be the best mum I could be to Lexie. No matter what I would make both of my girls proud of me. None of this hurt was going to be in vain. I didn't know what I was going to do but one thing I knew for sure, I wasn't going to be beaten.

Chapter 4

MY BABY DIED—
I DIDN'T LOSE HER

EVERYTHING WAS SO SURREAL. I WAS NOW A member of an exclusive club that I really didn't want to be a part of, the "angel mummy" club. The hospital allows loved ones to spend time with their babies before taking them to burial. I lay on the bed waiting for Layla's body to be brought to me. I had no idea what to expect. I didn't know how to react. I didn't know what to say. I just lay there in silence, numb and in shock.

I posted an announcement on Facebook that Layla was gone so that people would stop messaging me to ask how she was. I figured I would let everyone know at the same time and get it over and done with. I was crushed. I had lost my battle.

I opened the windows. It was freezing but I knew they were bringing a dead body into my room and I was afraid the temperature would affect her. It's strange the things you think about. I was still looking after her even though she was gone. I was still trying to prepare things for her. I was still her mum.

The sun was shining outside. I watched as people made their way to work and went about their usual business. It was a stark reminder that just because my world had stopped, the rest of the world was still turning. As I lay on the bed, one million thoughts went through my brain. I decided that I wasn't going to lose my mind. I had to keep fighting for Lexie. I couldn't let this take me down and I didn't want Layla to be a tragic thing that happened to me. I was proud of her. I was proud of the way she changed all our lives in such a short period of time. She was my beautiful baby girl.

So, I looked out the window and I said to myself, "I am going to beat this and I'm going to make both of my girls proud of me. I am going to do something and both are going to be so proud that I am their mummy. All this was not in vain." I kept repeating this, as it was the narrative I was telling myself—my mantra was to push through and get things done.

There was a knock at the door. She was here.

I looked at Layla lying in the Moses basket beside me. She was so cold. The nurses showed me how to hold her and suggested ways I could cuddle her. I was still afraid of hurting her, even though she was dead. I didn't want to injure her or break her.

I phoned a friend who was a funeral director and asked him if he would bury her. I was shaking as I phoned him and cried uncontrollably as I tried to speak. I managed to say, "My baby has died. Will you arrange her funeral?" Just as I said that, I began to cry so hard that I literally couldn't breathe. I had to just hang up.

The pain of losing a child is unbelievable. I had gotten pretty familiar with pain at this point, but this was different because my soul was crying. My heart had been ripped in two. My body was still pregnant, searching for the baby it had just carried full term while my brain was trying to make sense of what was going on.

Before leaving the hospital, I picked up my hospital bag and asked the nurse if there was anyone in the hospital who didn't have a lot of money and could use the items in the bag. She was really shocked by my question and told me, "You would be surprised at how many women are sex trafficked here. They are dropped off by their pimps and have nothing. Some go back to them, and some we manage to put into the system". I was horrified to think that this was happening on my doorstep. I asked the nurse to take the bag and give it to a mum she felt needed it.

I started making plans to leave the hospital without my baby. I was leaving with an empty tummy, empty heart, and an empty car seat. I decided the best way was to walk out and avoid making eye contact with people. I held my breath and put one foot in front of the other, bracing myself as I walked out past the reception area where all the expectant mums were. I knew I looked horrendous, like I had been in an accident. My eyes were huge with shock and tears. I just kept walking and looked at no one. I felt so alone in this. I knew I had to protect myself and be strong for Lexie. Stepping outside the hospital was strange. I had built myself so that once I stepped out those doors my life was never going to be the same again. But my reality looked the same as it did when I walked in the hospital. Except this time, my belly was empty.

On the way home I stopped into a children's dress shop to get a beautiful dress for Layla to be buried in. I picked out the pinkest, frilliest, fluffiest dress I could find. I didn't worry about the cost because I knew I would never buy clothes for her again. The lady in the shop asked me if my baby was being christened. I said, "No, she's being buried". The lady's face dropped. She was lovely and brought me a chair to sit on while I looked at the dresses. She gave Layla some free accessories. This may sound strange to some people but in that moment, I was still a mummy doing what I could for my child. Even though Layla wasn't with me, I still wanted to do all I could for her.

When I got home, I went straight to bed and cried. I cried and I cried. I stared at the wall and I cried some more. In a strange way it was good to feel the pain because at least I was feeling something. I couldn't hold my baby or love her, but I could feel that pain. It was a dangerous thought pattern.

The next day, my sickness was back with a vengeance. I walked downstairs and horror filled me. I wanted my baby girl. I wanted her so bad. I would do anything to hold her alive again.

I tried so hard to hold it together, but I was so ill. The pain was intolerable. The sickness was nonstop and the dizziness kept me lying down unable to move much. When I did move, I would vomit uncontrollably for forty-five minutes straight.

The day of Layla's funeral came.

I took a deep breath and held it, putting one foot in front of the other.

I didn't want to talk to people, simply because I didn't know if I could without bursting into tears. I requested that no one wear black, but that everyone wear bright colors. We released white doves and 25 balloons for each hour she was alive.

I tried not to make eye contact with anyone and just concentrated on breathing. I didn't want to have to deal with other people's awkward questions or comments. There is nothing in this life that will ever prepare you for losing a baby. I don't even like that expression because I wasn't careless. I didn't lose her. She died. It wasn't my fault. I did everything I could to save her but it just wasn't enough. Suddenly all those dreams of my two girls playing and growing up together were gone. I started to think of everyone that I might bump into and ask me how she was. I didn't want to talk to anyone. It was strange that I didn't want to talk to anyone, but I did want to scream from the rooftops, "MY BABY DIED!"

Most people do not know how to handle a mother whose child has died. Everyone gets so awkward and weird about things. Let me help you out: Talk to her like she is normal. If she talks about her baby, you talk too. She will appreciate that you acknowledged her child's existence. A grieving mother has already been to hell and back. There's nothing you can say that will kill her, so please do not isolate or avoid anyone you meet who has experienced the death of a child. You may provide just the conversation she needs to remind her that she is human and life is real.

The day of Layla's funeral was beautiful and sunny. I was relieved to get through it. In Ireland, it's normal to go to a bar to drink and party after a funeral. I went to a friend's house instead. Although I was desperately ill, I started to drink, thinking it might take away the pain. But it didn't. People kept hugging me and looking at me awkwardly. I just wanted to be treated normal. I just wanted to *be* normal. I felt exhausted, so I went up to my friend's bedroom. Still in the clothes I wore to Layla's funeral, I lay on her bed and cried. I could hear people chatting and just getting on with things downstairs while I was upstairs alone, trying not to fall apart.

When morning came, I woke up and walked around the house. I looked and felt such a state that I went back to bed and I just lay there trying to make sense of my life. Every few seconds I would vomit violently, a reminder that I was still in hell.

My mum came to see how I was doing and I just lost it. I screamed at her, "Why did your God kill my baby!" She looked at me in shock. I was so deeply hurt that I was screaming on the inside. Every part of me ached with a deep yearning for someone I couldn't have. It literally felt as though a part of my soul had been violently ripped out from me. None of this made any sense. I promised God that I would be a good Christian if He saved my baby, so why didn't He? Why didn't He stop this from happening? What kind of God allows this?

No one really understands the pain that comes with the death of a child unless they have been through it. Many people thought I should just be able to move on after the death of my baby, but it's not that easy. A part of me died the day that Layla left. I fought with everything I had to save her and she died. She was gone, and I wasn't getting her back.

One of the hardest questions to answer is "how many children do you have?" I often found myself preempting this question and changing the conversation quickly by pointing out something really obvious and mundane like the awful weather we always seem to have. Or if the question did manage to filter through, I would go into my own head and panic. How could I answer this without making them uncomfortable, honouring my baby and also managing not to cry? It took me several years and a lot of healing to get to the point where I could just say "I have one child and a baby in heaven as well" and be ok with their disappointed or empathetic expressions.

If you are reading this, and you are walking this awful road please take comfort in the fact, it does get easier. You can learn to breathe again. It took me some practice. As you will continue to read, I hit a lot of bumps in the road before I found the key to unlocking peace, overcoming grief and finally accepting myself. Learn from this journey. You can give power to my pain by learning from my mistakes and processes and ultimately hopefully, save you or someone close to you from going through the same.

My symptoms increased, and my body deteriorated massively. Life was unbearable. Six weeks after Layla's death the neurosurgical team admitted me for emergency brain surgery. They warned me that this Foramen Magnum Decompression surgery was one of the worst in terms of recovery. They had to open the back of my head to remove a part of my skull and vertebrae. The surgery was awful. I was in that much pain and had such sensitivity to light and sound, the other patients on the ward had to sit in the dark and not make a sound while I lay in bed screaming in pain with sunglasses on.

I couldn't move. The pain was ten times worse than anything I had experienced. My back and limbs ached from being in the same position for so long and I was still vomiting violently. How could this be my life? My baby had just died and here I am suffering in a way no one should. I was so fed up; I knew there had to be more to my life. This wasn't my end. Somehow, I would get past this. Something on the inside kept pushing me on.

I wouldn't allow Lexie to visit me because I didn't want her to see me in so much pain, unable to move. My heart ached so badly. As I lay in the bed trying to rest, I heard the commotion of people walking. They had a baby with them. I was not prepared for this. Children are not generally allowed on the neurosurgery ward. I started to panic. My gut was wrenched. The baby started to cry and a terrifying wail came out of me, an uncontrollable cry. I couldn't stop it and I was very aware everyone could hear me. All of the nurses knew that my baby had died six weeks earlier. When I asked one of the nurses to close my curtains so that I could have privacy, she told me to "shut up crying".

Even in the hospital I was treated like I was worthless and I was totally incapable of defending myself. I had no choice but to just lie there crying my heart sore, watching this family with their baby while mine was cold in the ground. After about three weeks I started to make plans to go home. I worked hard with the physical therapists to get walking again. My focus was getting home to Lexie. The surgery left a large wound up the back of my head. My hair was shaved in the back, so I had to wear pig tails. I looked like someone had cracked me in the back of a head with a hatchet. It was safe to say I was going nowhere when I got home. I needed rest.

On the day I returned home from the

hospital, the rain poured out of the heavens. It matched my mood entirely. I flicked on the TV to see a flood warning for our area. The rains came in torrents until my entire road was flooded right up to the window-sill outside my house. I tried to grab whatever I could from the downstairs floor. Just as I got onto the stairs with Lexie, a fire engine drove up my street and created a wave that knocked down the wall outside my house and jarred my front door open. Lexie screamed and cried as the water came in. As I stood on the stairs with Lexie, all I could think of was what was happening to Layla's body in the ground. I didn't care about the house; I cared about my baby.

How much more could a girl take? This was just another huge event that could have broken me. I had to get back on track some-how. I figured that if I kept moving, I could get through all the pain. If I could just get to one goal, I could reach another. I was making things up as I went along, but I had to do something.

My best friend at the time had organized a party at his house and invited a medium.

The event had been booked just before I had Layla and there were no spaces left. As luck would have it, someone dropped out. I could go and see the medium.

What a crazy time that was. I went into the bedroom with the medium. Her mum wrote down the reading for each guest. I sat there as she began to talk to spirits. I was hugely skeptical but interested, nevertheless. As a new grieving mum, any sign of reassurance about Layla would have been awesome, but I knew enough about the Bible to know that if this woman was talking about our dead loved ones, they were probably in hell.

I watched intently as this lady began talking to spirits. She told me things about my life that she couldn't have known. She spoke about my family and my future. Sure enough she got some things right, but she also got a lot of it wrong. Way wrong. The whole experience was bizarre. I observed her closely to see if she was acting or legitimately speaking to someone. She was talking to someone or something all right. I had no doubt about that. This medium was very well known and was booked up for months in advance. She drove a large flashy car and had just come back from an expensive holiday. She was living the high life, so it would seem.

The medium's mum gave me my reading and I took it home and stuffed it in a drawer. What a load of nonsense.

My health started to take a bad turn. I just couldn't get a grip on things. At this point, my short-term memory was so severely damaged that at times I didn't even know my name. One time, I went to the local garage just four doors from my house. When I got there, my mind went completely blank. I forgot who I was, where I was, what I was doing. I didn't know anything. I fell to the floor and one of the attendants who knew me gathered me up and took me home.

To outsiders, I looked like I wasn't going to make it, but I knew there was more ahead of me. Don't ask me how, but I just knew this wasn't my end. My life became a constant whirlwind of hospital visits desperately seeking relief. I have lost count of how many times I crawled into the hospital. I was admitted so many times that they didn't even bother treating me, but sent me home in the same state I arrived. I couldn't understand why they were not helping me. Why they weren't making me better. Medical staff walked past me during rounds in the hospital ward, leaving me there in pain and doubt. One morning I couldn't take it anymore and I cried out, "Please help me. My baby has just died and my other baby needs me. Please help me!" They looked at me and just said, "Sorry, you aren't our patient," and walked on. My doctor never came.

I have never counted how many trips we had to the hospital in that period but I would not be surprised if it was heading towards a thousand. My mum and stepdad were exhausted and drained from having to look after me and Lexie. They endured all the ups and downs of my emergencies, sitting in the waiting rooms for up to twelve hours, only for me to be turned away or admitted for one night and sent home with no treatment. The financial burden was severe. Long-term sickness was expensive.

Something had to change. I was living well below the poverty line and constantly robbing Peter to pay Paul. Bills were mounting up and I just couldn't seem to catch a break. I had to do something that would give me a bit of freedom and also put some money in the bank. I needed a long-term goal and a plan for the future, so I signed up to go back to college to study Forensic Science. I was determined to do this, no matter what.

Chapter 5

I GIVE UP, I GIVE IN

EVERYONE AROUND ME WAS SHOCKED TO learn I planned to return to college. Even with everything else I had going on, I knew it was the right choice. It gave me something else to focus on besides my troubles and gave me hope for the future. I didn't know how I would survive each day; I was just winging it. My neurosurgeon told me I would live a life of pain and survive on benefits, so I should just get used to it.

Face palm to myself.

There I had it, doctor's orders! It didn't matter what hell I was in, I just needed to get on with it. I somehow translated this to "let's go and get wasted." It wasn't even a destructive need. I just wanted to feel normal. I needed an outlet, something in my life that wasn't centered around brain surgery or death, something that was just fun.

I didn't consider the fact that I was seriously emotionally impacted by the events of my entire life up to now. I didn't see that

I had serious mental health issues like depression, anxiety and suicidal thoughts. I was masking. Trying to completely avoid and compress the darkness that was lurking within me. If I could just do the things that everyone else was doing. If I could put up a front to convince others that all was well with me, I figured I would be all right. As long as I kept up a brave face that no one needed to know I was crying myself to sleep. That real "ugly" crying where your face is screwed up beyond recognition and your nose is running down your chin but you are so paralysed with grief that you can't get up to get a tissue. That was my nighttime ritual. But no one knew. Hey, I had my demons and I had to learn to live with them? Right? Wrong! For reasons you will read about later.

What can you do when everything else is against you? For me, the answer was to go and get wasted. Yes, I was still sick, but I needed to feel normal. I bought a new dress, got my hair done, booked a makeup artist and started to look like myself again. I felt human. I was determined that I was going out and no one or nothing on this planet was going to stop me. I was going to have fun even if it killed me! So in my normal fashion, I hit the bar. The drink hit me and off I went. I was having a great time. No awkward questions, no hassles. It was just me, the music and as many shots as I could get my hands on. After the club, we all went back to a friend's house. Everyone drank way more than they should have and had things they shouldn't have, if you get me. We were all just enjoying the night. I went up to the restroom. When I came out, a girl named Tracey called me into the bedroom. She was crying. I asked her what was wrong. "Every time I look at you, I think of dead babies," she said. I was stunned and didn't know what to say. I found myself trying to console her. I genuinely didn't know what to do. I wanted to keep enjoying myself, but the girl was crying uncontrollably. As I walked down the stairs, one of the other girls asked, "What's wrong with Tracey?" I shared what Tracey told me and immediately a group of girls ran up the stairs to check on her, but no one ran to help me.

An older woman screamed in my face,

"See you, Stephanie, bringing all of your drama in here!" Before I knew it, a full scale argument erupted with me being the bad guy. My "friends" threw me out of the house. I was outside, drunk, alone, and crying inconsolably. I didn't understand what happened. I had done nothing, yet I was being accused and everything seemed to erupt against me. I couldn't get home quick enough.

Once I slept off my hangover, I decided that it was game face on. Then some kind of supernatural force gave me a kick up the backside that I needed. I didn't want to be depressed and lonely. I didn't want to be a mess. My goodness, I had this wonderful, beautiful, funny child and I needed to get myself together for her. I had no time to waste. I needed to get our lives on track for her sake.

I threw myself into my college work and condensed the two-year course into one year. My tutors were awesome. I was still battling chronic sickness and at times I had to hold onto the walls to walk. I just kept going. Completing all my assessments and assignments, I achieved the highest possible marks. This was more than enough to get into University. Things were finally looking up. I could do this.

It was summertime and I was on a high from beating the odds in spite of all my neurosurgeon's dark predictions. I jumped into a taxi and went to our top university and headed to the law department. Once I reached the offices, I asked if I could come "do a wee law degree". The lady at the desk looked me up and down with a mixture of horror and disgust. "Do you realize this is June and our admissions are in January? You can't just waltz in here off the street. What grades do you have anyway?" As you can imagine, my preferred response would have been to tell her to shove it, but I needed this. So I replied, "Would three *A*s be acceptable for you?" She almost choked. I could see she was quite taken back. "Well if you can prove those grades, we would certainly welcome an application like yours". I could see her words were causing her great pain. I loved it.

Though I was incredibly tempted to ram it down her throat, I calmly gave her my transcript as proof of my grades and within days I had an unconditional offer for three law degrees. I was so happy! Nothing could bring me down now.

I was still on this continual loop of going back and forth to the hospital and begging for help—and still no one would help me. On one trip to the hospital, I met a temporary consultant from Leeds. He couldn't believe the state I was in or how I was able to survive so long on the VP shunt device that surgeons had implanted. I could barely stand. I was falling all over the place. He knew he had to help me or I was going to die.

My mum and I were excited that we finally found a doctor who would help us. He admitted me and ran lots of tests, including several lumbar punctures. No one is excited about a lumbar puncture, but I was so happy to be one step closer to getting the help I needed. The doctor booked me for emergency surgery to implant a shunt in my brain.

I woke up with half of my head shaved. I was groggy but not as bad as I usually was. Immediately, I could feel the relief. I felt like I could be normal again. I had hope.

I threw myself into studying law. I honestly hated it. I felt so out of place and out of sorts. But I was not a quitter, so I kept going.

I started to get sick again. I couldn't believe this was happening. I had about five months of relief and now it felt like I was back at square one. I had unbearable headaches and temporary paralysis that caused facial drooping and slurred speech. I had no choice but to quit university. I was just a complete mess. It was typical, just as my life was going somewhere, it screwed up again.

Without the help of the consultant from Leeds, we were back to running the health service gauntlet. Why was this always happening to me? Why couldn't they just treat me and help me? I turned my anger toward God.

I had Lexie to feed and clothe, a house I needed to run, and now no university funds were coming through. Things got desperate. So many times, I only had money to buy food for Lexie and had to borrow money to pay the electric bill. I needed more than this out of life. Lexie needed and deserved more.

I had £5 left to my name and little food. We walked past four houses to get to the ga-

rage when I saw a beautiful flower arrange-
ment suitable for a child's grave. Anyone that
has a child in heaven will tell you how hard
it is to get suitable arrangements. I broke
down in tears because I promised Lexie a
magazine for being a good girl, but I didn't
have enough money to buy the magazine
and the flowers. I felt like my legs were going
to give way. How could my life have gotten
to this point? I had to choose between buy-
ing a magazine for my living child or flowers
for my dead child. This needed to change. I
needed to change. I had to do something.

A local lady had been in touch with me
to join a network marketing company. I had
heard some negative things about network
marketing. For someone in my position, who
did not know how they would live from one
day to the next, it was a lifeline that I needed.
I phoned her, got the details, and borrowed
£69.00 to join. I made an inner decision that
I was going to give it my all and make money
out of this.

This inner decision was so important. I
knew that if I were to achieve any kind of
goal or endeavor, I needed to fully commit.

I decided on my success and acted like I already achieved it!

I became a student of success, devouring YouTube videos, audiobooks, and stalking people who were successful. I got into my bath with a sick bucket beside me and I learned everything I could about social media marketing, personal development, and leadership.

I started selling on Facebook and building a sales team. I pushed through my sickness and taught sales skills to women from around the world. I even conducted live seminars on Facebook from a hospital bed. I threw everything I had and more into that company and sure enough within eighteen months, I generated approximately £2M in sales, leading a team of women from nine countries around the world. I had a wonderful team of women that I genuinely loved. My fire was lit, and my heart was full. I was on a mission.

I knew what it was like to be so broke I didn't have enough money to feed myself. I knew what it was like to sit in the house without the TV on because I was trying to save electricity.

By mastering network marketing and teaching sales I found a way that I could give back. I found the thing I was meant to do. I was born to teach. I loved helping other women earn money and inspiring people to create an income from home. I wasn't receiving any government assistance or benefits. I was fully supporting myself and Lexie and I could afford holidays, treats, and clothes. I was experiencing financial freedom. If only I could get free of chronic migraines and sickness. If only I could be well again.

Every day was like living in a constant state of emergency, and we were all exhausted from it. I kept building my business and trying to create a life for Lexie, not knowing if I would live or die. Sometimes I would lie in bed, and it would feel like it was lifting. The walls seemed as if they were falling on top of me. I really thought I was losing it.

I couldn't understand why the doctors wouldn't fix me. I couldn't understand why they saw me as a nuisance and as a person who was suffering and in need of help.

Sometimes they would roll their eyes when they saw me, sometimes they would flat out scream at me, "You have to stop this! You need to learn to live like that!"

But I couldn't. How could this be normal? How could anyone accept this constant pain and misery as a way of life. I just *knew* there was a way out of this. I *knew* something or someone could help me. But the doctors saw me as a waste of time. Nothing they could do was going to "fix me," so spending anytime speaking to me was a waste of their precious time. It all became too much. All my life I was treated like I was worthless and beneath everyone. I was constantly battling grief. I had enough.

I decided I was better off dead. I couldn't live like this anymore. What was the point of me stretching out this suffering? It was better that I end it all and do everyone a favor. I walked upstairs and collected all of the heavy-duty neuro pain meds I had. Sitting on the landing, I opened the bottle and swallowed all of the pills. Everything went blank.

Bill had been downstairs with Lexie. He knew what I was doing. He knew exactly what I was doing. As I lay dying on the floor, he decided to leave me to die. He walked out and left me on the floor as life was leaving my body. He didn't call an ambulance. He just left me to die.

The next thing I remembered was waking up with a tube down my throat. My mum and stepdad stood by my bed. I panicked and tried to pull the tube out because I was choking. A nurse grabbed my hands, and I became unconscious again.

Later I learned that I had been in a coma. I survived.

How I was found was quite miraculous. A friend who was also a nurse, decided to call my house. When she didn't get an answer, she came to my house. The door was unlocked. She found me upstairs and called the ambulance. She saved my life.

This was a wakeup call. I needed help.

When I woke up from that coma, I was glad. I wasn't embarrassed at what I had done, I was glad I had survived, but I knew I had to get help. I needed something to help me straighten out my life and more importantly my head.

My mum had been pestering me about going to church. No, thank you! I'd had enough of church to last me a lifetime.

Everyone was talking about this book called *The Secret* by Rhonda Byrne. I watched people online manifesting joy, great things in their lives, and even handbags because they had begun to practice the advice given in the book. It seemed it had something I needed too. The more I looked into it, the more attractive it seemed. I bought the book, excited about the prospect of it, I watched the movie online too. It was free and didn't involve me having to stand in a church and sing. It was like another Bible story, as the movie seems very biblical. The characters are dressed how you imagine biblical characters and it uses language to help guide you about love and power. Something just wasn't sitting right with me. It made me feel creepy. Like I was a young child watching an adult movie, I couldn't describe it but I just knew there was something very wrong about that movie. The more I listened to it, the more I thought it was a load of nonsense. I brushed it off. Alert! Failed attempt at redirecting my life.

Then things started to get really weird.

Chapter 6

MIRACLES REALLY
DO HAPPEN

AFTER YOU TRY TO KILL YOURSELF, IT'S all a bit surreal. My suicide attempt wasn't a cry for help or attention. I fully intended to end my life. My partner did nothing to stop me or help me. Somehow, I lived to tell this.

Once I came around, I regretted what I did and was glad that I hadn't succeeded. I really loved my wee Lexie. I loved her so much. She needed me.

I haven't really spoken about this until now. It was a secret shame of mine. I didn't want people knowing I had lost it so bad and I didn't want them thinking I was an attention seeker. I avoided talking about it at all costs. I share it now because I believe my story will help people.

When you are in a dark place of nothingness, it feels like the only way out is in a box. I know what it's like to feel alone with no one to call. I know the frustration of trying everything and failing. You feel like every breath you take is robbing someone else of theirs.

I needed to do something. Years had passed by now and I was still in this limbo, in this never-ending season of pain and torment. This could not be how life is meant to be. There had to be something else. There had to be an answer beyond me because I was running out of ideas at how I could save myself from drowning in my own circumstance again. I was open to trying anything at this point. I needed to find my place in the world. There had to be something that would make things "click" for me.

My mum arrived to take me for a coffee. I could barely stand but made the effort. Once I got settled into the car, she handed me an ancient CD player and insisted that there was a man she saw at church the night before that I needed to hear. I pressed play.

I was immediately outraged! A man that I knew nothing about was talking about me in a church. Screaming at my mum, I turned the CD player off and threw it in the back of the car. How dare she go around and tell my business to people I didn't know. Steam was coming out of my ears.

Mum was persistent. A couple of days later, she appeared at my door excitedly, talking about a man who had a healing ministry. Millions of people had been healed through his ministry. I dreaded the idea of going to church but I was curious and desperate to be healed. At this stage in my life I couldn't afford to be choosy. It was worth a shot.

Having no idea what to expect, I prepared myself to go to this church. I had been in a lot of churches growing up. I knew that if this church was like any of those, there was no way I was getting healed. I was so ill I looked like I had been run over by a car and I couldn't stand upright. I wondered what people would think of me. The people at the church seemed nice enough but I was highly suspicious that they would try to suck me into their church lifestyle, so I avoided conversations with them. I didn't need to be saved. I didn't need church. I just needed to be healed so I could get on with my life. It was that simple.

One of the ladies in the church asked

if we were coming to church the following week to hear Alejandro Arias, the "Boy
Preacher" with a huge healing anointing. I
could not believe it. My mum had brought
me on the WRONG night.

I sat with a face like stone. The music began. I started to pay a little attention
but I made sure no one saw me. I started to
feel good. I could almost smile. The whole
church had their hands in the air and I immediately thought, "There is no way I'm doing that!" This was different than any church
I had been in before. Yes, something was
very different here.

As the music continued to play, I could
hear people speaking some kind of gibberish.
I didn't understand why they were talking
through the worship. I grew up in a church
where you couldn't even look sideways during the hymns. The music was pumping. It
was as good as a lot of concerts I had been to.
The atmosphere here was so different.

I looked up, convinced they were pumping acid in through the ceiling. It just wasn't
normal for this many people to be smiling
and happy in church. Something weird was

going on here and I was going to find out what it was.

When we left the church, I screamed at my mum for bringing me to a cult. Had I not been through enough? Had I not suffered enough? I didn't need her weird friends sucking me into a church and boring me to death.

Something very dark was going on at home. At night, when I was sleeping, I could feel my bed shaking. Each time I got up to go to the restroom I had this awful gut wrenching feeling that something was following me. I could almost sense someone watching me. I started sleeping with the hall light on. I dreaded night time.

The following week we arrived to the church to see Alejandro Arias, "The Boy Preacher." I had never seen anything like it. The worship music began and I could see people shaking. I thought they were having fits. Everyone had their arms up, worshipping. Two women were shaking violently and fell to the floor. No one pushed them.

I was both intrigued and suspicious. What was this?

Alejandro shared his testimony and it all sounded great, but how was he going to help me? If no one in the medical profession could help me, how was he going to help?

He called for anyone who wanted to receive prayer to go up to the front. I looked at my mum, frightened. Before I could give her an excuse she firmly said, "Get up there, now!" Like a good girl, I obeyed.

I stood in the prayer line. The worship music was loud and everyone was excited, except me. I was terrified. What if he pushed me to the ground and I died? What if I didn't fall over and they attacked me? I watched as people fell to the floor, but the preacher wasn't pushing them. What on earth was going on? He just spoke to them and they fell over. I was petrified. What was this?

My legs started to bend. I looked up at my mum and said, "Oh, Mummmyyy."

She laughed and then he prayed for her and down she went. Just like that.

Before I had time to panic, he came to me. I didn't even feel his hand touch me, but I could smell this amazing fragrance. I felt really warm and happy. It felt better than any high I had ever experienced. I didn't even catch what he said. I was just in complete bliss and happiness. Then I felt a *BOOM*, and I knew I was going down. Someone caught me and laid me down gently. I laid there and smiled for the first time in a long time.

This was real. This had actually happened. Why hadn't anyone told me about this before now? This actually works! I felt good! I felt a love that was hard to describe. It was something you had to experience to understand. I now know it was joy and peace. I immediately realized that I wasn't in pain. This really worked! Success! Freedom! It was time to party. I had already started to mentally arrange my outfits, planning to go out and get wasted. Then I thought, *Wait. Since I was healed in a church, I wonder if I have to keep going.*

The people I met in church were so excited about the change in me. I really had received a miracle. I could stand without stumbling. I didn't feeling sick and I had no pain. It was a miracle! At the end of the service I went up to tell Alejandro what happened. I didn't want him to know I wasn't saved, so I quickly told my story and tried to leave. Just as I was skulking away, a woman told him I wasn't saved. He called me back and said, "Are you really not a Christian? Would you like to receive Jesus as your Lord and Savior?" Normally all kinds of alarm bells would have been going off in me, but before I knew it, I was praying the prayer of salvation with him. I did it. I did the thing I swore I would never do. I gave my life to the Lord.

I immediately felt a shift. It was hard to put into words, but I knew my whole life had just changed. Everyone was so happy for me and congratulated me. I was happy for me. I wasn't in pain. I walked outside and was almost blinded by the sun. I knew it was a sign from God that I had stepped out of darkness and into light.

The sky seemed so blue and the grass was so green. The birds were singing. It was like I was seeing the world for the first time. I walked up a road I had traveled thousands of times but now it was like I was seeing it for the first time.

My mum was delighted. She gave me the

world's biggest Bible. I wasn't ready for all of the jumping around, hand waving, clapping, and singing. I was in, but I was still very cautious. All of this was new to me. I had so many questions. How did I know the Holy Spirit was even real? How was He able to knock me to the floor and heal me from the disabilities the doctors couldn't? This caused me to evaluate everything in my life.

It was like finding out the Matrix was real. I lived my whole life believing a load of lies. Now that I had received the truth, so much stuff started to make sense. Things were clicking into place all around me. It was amazing.

Up to this point I had been dependent on sleeping tablets to sleep at night. They weren't the heavy duty ones, just natural tablets to help me drift off. Without them I wouldn't sleep at all. I had tried many times to come off of them but it never worked.

The day after I got saved, I started to take one of my sleeping tablets as I had always done. I felt this prompting not to take them, so I didn't and I have never taken another sleeping tablet. I really do believe this was another healing I received. Now I sleep so deeply it would take a bomb to wake me.

The darkness at home went to a whole other level. Nighttime was the worst. In addition to my bed shaking, I sensed an evil presence in my room. I didn't know what to do. I couldn't scream because I didn't want to wake Lexie. I was stunned into silence and terrified. This wasn't just my imagination. I thought of every possible explanation to make sense of this. Something was at work in my house and it wasn't a good thing. I started to cry. I cried out to God. I remembered hearing in the church that worship music changed the atmosphere, so I grabbed my phone and searched for Christian worship music. I didn't even know any worship songs. The first song that came up was "No Longer Slaves". I pressed play and closed my eyes, inwardly begging God to do something. The shaking stopped and I fell asleep.

Lots of weird things started happening. TV started changing channels on its own and the lights would go out without warning. My bed continued to shake at night. It was like living in a horror movie. I have never been into the occult, so I didn't really know anything about demons. I had never even considered if they were real. Something was fighting against me and I didn't know what it was. My mum had no doubts at all that it was the devil coming against me because I had become a Christian.

Wait a minute! I didn't sign up for any of this. What did she mean the devil was coming against me? I got saved and agreed to go to church. Surely that was enough.

I had barely wrapped my mind around the fact Jesus was alive, that He really healed, and He was coming back. Now I was being bullied by demons in my home! I couldn't tell any of my friends. How could I bring this up in conversation without sounding like a lunatic?

Strange things started happening to my body, too. Painful muscle spasms caused my fingers and arms to curl and contort. We sought medical help but we knew this was a demonic attack.

I thought maybe if I prayed, whatever was in the house would go away. I prayed out loud, not really knowing what to say. I just began to say, "Jesus, Jesus, Jesus. Help me, Lord."

I could feel darkness coming over the house. I went upstairs into the spare bedroom and found a swarm of flies from nowhere. There hadn't been any food or anything rotting. I could see shapes of huge demons in the shadows. My bed was lifting off the floor every night. Everything inside me was screaming there was something wrong. Something evil was here. I was way out of my depth.

My mum and I prayed and asked God to send us someone who could help us. Most nights I would text her and she would pick us up to go stay at her house.

This was truly off the scale. It was nuts!

Seriously, had I not been through enough? Now I had to fight demons? I screamed at my mum, "What have you done? Why is this happening to me?"

In my back living room, I had a large gambling machine just like you see in a bar. It was my money box. One day as I walked toward the living room, I heard a loud BANG. The front door of the machine flew off and I saw a dragon shaped shadow fly out. It flew past me onto the upstairs landing. All the electricity in the house blew out. I ran as fast as I could.

Who do you call when you are up against a demon? Ghostbusters won't cut it! My mum and I prayed and prayed. Then, my mum had a chance meeting or divine appointment with a pastor that she knew from my dad's Bible school days. His name was David Legge. He had a deliverance ministry. I had never heard of deliverance, but my mum knew exactly what it was and assured me it was just what we needed.

David asked me to contact him with a breakdown of everything that had been going on. I sent the email and soon after he contacted me to make the first appointment.

I had no idea what deliverance was or what this man could do, but he was the only option I had.

Chapter 7

DEMONS ARE REAL

I SET OFF TO GO TO DAVID'S HOUSE. HIS wife agreed to meet me at the train station and drive me to their home. I was a little scared but ultimately I felt it was the right thing to do. I had a peace that this was a major key to stopping all this crazy stuff from happening to us. It couldn't get much worse, could it?

When I arrived at their lovely home, they offered me a drink and reassured me that deliverance was nothing weird and they were just going to pray for me. They were used to dealing with people that had a lot of demonic activity in their lives. I think it's important at this point to clarify that deliverance is a Christian practice and is in alignment with Scripture. If you feel that you need a deliverance minister, make sure you find a reputable one who knows what to do.

David prayed for protection for us and for the house. As he prayed, my arms started to curl and contort. Every muscle in my body seized up. I had no control over my own body. I was aware of what was happening but I had no control whatsoever. My legs started kicking and my body jerking. David commanded the demon to come out of me.

Then, I began to speak. It was my mouth and my voice but it wasn't me that was talking. It was a demon. The demon told David that it was going to kill me. It said that there were legions of demons spilling out of the gates of hell onto the earth and to get ready because they were going to kill us all.

At this point I was on the floor, my whole body convulsing. I couldn't do anything to stop anything. The movements were so severe that I was moving around the room. David continued to pray, anointing me with oil. He repeated scriptures and commanded the demon to leave. After a short time, I felt a release. Then I began to vomit violently. Something like a black tar came out of me. I was so relieved. In a strange way, I felt a bit cleaner on the inside. Something dark had left me.

When the session was over I asked David, "Am I possessed?"

He looked a little nervous and said, "I more prefer the term *demonized*. But, Stephanie you are saved now and walking with the Lord, so freedom is yours. But, I'll be honest. I've never met anyone that the demons are so determined to kill."

That was typical for me.

David prepared me by telling me that deliverance was going to be a process. He explained it like a tree's root system. "If you want to take down a tree in your garden," he said, "you need to get to the roots and there are many."

I felt as if I had been run over by a bus. Every part of me ached but I felt lighter, like something had shifted. This was easy. I could do this! Or so I thought.

Now I knew what I was dealing with. I was getting a crash course in casting out demons and deliverance. I had more confidence that I could be set free. This was serious stuff but Jesus died on the cross and His blood was spilled to give me the authority to command these demons to go.

When I got home the demons in my house stepped up a gear, but I wasn't afraid.

I had confidence that with God on my side I would get through this. God was taking me on a journey. He had brought me this far, I wasn't going to die now!

At night I could hear something scurrying around, but not on the floor. It sounded like it was in the walls and a lot bigger than a mouse. I followed the sound and it seemed to go from my room into the one beside mine, but stayed in the wall. It was a horrible noise and it really creeped me out. I will never forget it.

My mum and I had decided to try and cleanse my house ourselves. We started upstairs because that was where most of the demonic activity was. The darkness was almost tangible. It was like the demons were watching us and waiting to see what we would do. This was a thousand times creepier than walking down a dark alley or past a graveyard. We entered each room with oil and prayed. The atmosphere shifted immediately. We walked into my bathroom and as my mum began to pray, I was bent over in half. I thought my spine was going to snap. My mum kept reading the prayer. We had to do this. We couldn't let the enemy take an inch. This was my house and the devil had no authority to torment me like this. I was taking my house back and sending those demons back to wherever they came from.

As we continued to pray, there were demonic manifestations in every room. It seemed my whole house was crawling in demons. It certainly explained a lot. We phoned David to ask for more help.

The second session at David's house was different. The Holy Spirit started to show him things I needed to repent of. These were sins or actions that I needed to acknowledge and ask God to forgive. People don't realize how small things can open up doors to the demonic in their lives. You don't have to be an axe murderer; if you ever lied, stole, had sex with someone you weren't married to, watched a horror movie, or took drugs you have potentially opened a door to the demonic in your life. Even a lot of contemporary music is created by people who have sold their soul. They don't even hide it. A lot of the language used in these songs refer to devil worship. So when you are dancing and singing to it, you are reveling and unwittingly coming into agreement with the devil. It's so subtle that people don't realize it. I know I didn't, until my eyes were opened and I saw the truth. I now understood the reason I kept going back to a toxic and abusive relationship was because there was a soul tie created through a sexual relationship. Even the sins my partner committed had a spiritual impact on me because our souls were tied together. It was something that had to be broken by the power of God.

The devil is sneaky, he isn't playing around. I had no idea all this stuff was at work in my life. I thought I just had bad luck. It was worse; I had demons. It is the enemy's agenda to send as many people to hell as possible so he devises schemes to entice people. Some people receive and accept open invitations; others like me are sucked in and tormented.

As David prayed, a different demon began to speak out of me. The language was unbelievable and certainly not something I could have thought up. My body was out of control and my legs swung about wildly.

I was growling and gnashing on the floor. The more David prayed, the worse it seemed to get. The atmosphere in the room was intense. At one point I lunged forward to bite him in the face, but he moved back. David took me through a series of prayers to repent for various things. I could feel a release but there was still something still there. It was a strongman. It was something much bigger that needed to go.

Once the session was over we explained what was happening in my house. David agreed to come and cleanse my home. In the meantime, he instructed me to go home and get rid of anything in the house that was not of God.

Immediately, the letter from the medium popped into my head. I asked David if that would be important. His eyes popped open, "Yes! Get that out of your house!" He went on to explain that even books, videos or anything related to the demonic or witchcraft had to go. This meant getting rid of all the Harry Potter videos, which were vessels of witchcraft disguised as children's books. I know this is not a popular view with a lot of people, but I'm not here to make friends. I'm here to tell you the truth. People need to know the truth and recognize deception to begin to get free. Whether you agree with me or not it's true. I wouldn't want my child or any child reciting those spells or playing with a wand. What many consider innocent children's books are straight from hell. The devil isn't going to walk up to your door and politely knock. He invites himself in through back doors like films, music, drugs, alcohol, and other ways. In the days we are living in, you have to be aware of these things.

I found out the gambling machine was also a doorway to the demonic spirit realm and made arrangements to get it removed from my house. For three months, every time we tried to have the machine removed, the enemy tried to stop it. The moving van broke down. The movers brought the wrong equipment. There was a mix up with my bookings. At one point, the machine came on by itself even though it was not connected to electricity. We finally lifted it and put it outside ourselves. I believe someone stole it. God help them, is all I can say. Christians should not gamble because it has spiritual implications. God isn't trying to ruin your fun. He is protecting you.

After I got rid of everything I could think of, David came to cleanse my house. Even after I removed everything I could think of, there was still something tormenting me. The attacks were off the scale. Every day and night, something weird and supernatural happened. David brought another man with him. He was immediately led by the Holy Spirit into the bedroom beside mine where I heard the scurrying sounds in the walls. David walked directly to a cupboard on top of a built in wardrobe. I had never opened it and I hadn't told David about it either. He opened the cupboard and found a bag filled with personal belongings and little trinkets with our names on them. I didn't put them there. I knew it was witchcraft. Someone was using these things to hurt us. I grabbed it and put it straight into a bag to be burned. Finding something like that was such a shock. From that day on, I didn't hear scurrying in the walls again.

As we went around my house, I could

feel the intensity. The devil was there, and he was ready for a fight.

When we got into my living room and as my body began to contort, I sat on the sofa and a demon named Jezebel began to talk through me. She taunted the ministers and my mum with slick jokes and sly comments. I wanted it to stop but I couldn't speak. I couldn't do anything. Inside I was thinking, *Jesus, Jesus, Jesus.* I believe that is why I was protected.

My mum lunged towards me to grab the demon but I flew back in the seat. Everyone kept praying. The more they prayed the angrier Jezebel got. She was losing. I could hear her rage as she spat at them and used vulgar language. Then, suddenly I felt a release. She was gone. I was exhausted.

People look at Christians and see them as judgmental extremists. If only they knew the truth. If only they knew the reality and danger of the demonic spirit realm. I learned so many ways the devil tried to kill me. God had been there my whole life. The solution for all of my problems was always Jesus Christ.

We had one more session at David's. This time he invited an eighty-year-old minister who had extensive experience in deliverance. He explained that he had half of Ireland praying with us. Everyone congregated in the living room. I asked if I could use the bathroom before we got started. When I got to the living room, the door bounced back as if I had hit an invisible force field. I was lifted up into the air and landed on the floor. Whatever it was did not want me going back into that room. I couldn't stand, so I crawled my way into the living room. I was determined to get free. I was fed up of being bullied and pushed around. I pushed forward even though my own body was trying to hold me back. My hip twisted out of socket and I couldn't move. The minister instantly identified it as voodoo. Someone had a voodoo doll of me with a pin in the hip. I thought my hip was going to break out of socket by a force I couldn't see. The minister said a prayer to remove it and I felt a release. I was so glad.

People make lighthearted jokes about voodoo, but it's very real and is even prevalent in children's cartoons. We make light hearted jokes about it. Here, I thought my hip was going to be broken out of the socket by a force I couldn't see.

This session was tough. My whole body contorted and convulsed, but I knew it was bringing me freedom. With each session, I saw massive changes in areas of my life including physical and mental health, my finances, and my friendships.

I didn't understand why I had never heard of deliverance before. Why was this not common practice? I believe the devil has made a lot of Christians either afraid of it or ignorant to it. This is the time that the Holy Spirit is bringing about massive change and we will begin to see a lot more people being set free.

This isn't weird or spooky stuff. This is real and it could save your life.

Just weeks before my deliverance I wanted nothing to do with God, but here I was with no doubts that He was real. Jesus is real. The Holy Spirit is real. Angels are real. The devil is real too, and so are demons. It's all real but we have been fooled into believing a lot of lies. Here is the truth: If you don't accept Jesus as your Lord and Savior, you ARE going to hell. That's not something you want to play around with.

Wouldn't it be much better to live the rest of your life being the best you can be by allowing God to use you to make an impact on your family, your city, and your nation? Wouldn't you rather be the one that broke out of the poverty cycle, that beat cancer, and destroyed marital divorce thread in your family? This is where I was—standing victorious and telling the world that I was made whole by the power of my God.

As I sit and type this chapter, I can tell you that I am totally free of pain and sickness. Jesus healed me of all trauma, depression and anxiety. What would have happened if I had not said yes to God? I would be dead now and in hell.

If you are reading this and you haven't given your life to the Lord, I urge you to do it today. What is the worst that can happen to you? If you will wholeheartedly say yes to God, He will wholeheartedly set you free and on the path you were destined to walk in.

So many of us were born as a target for demonic attack because the devil knows the plans God has for our lives. The enemy can see those who are marked for greatness and he does his best to take them out. While you will always face trials, you are so much stronger when you face them with God. He will not only bring you out on the other side but he will use trials to promote you and bring Him glory.

You only need to watch the news or scan social media to see the state of the world. It doesn't take a genius to figure out that we can't continue on this path. The reality is Jesus is coming back. It won't be long.

If you are not walking with God, you are not fulfilling your destiny. I would not be sharing all my trials and tragedies with you if there wasn't a serious reason for it. You are here for a reason.

Anyone who looks at me today would not believe the details of my past. Those who knew me before can see the transformation in my life. I am not the same person I was. I even look different. I'm not a perfect person. I have done a lot of wrong things and have hurt people. But because of what Jesus did on the cross, I am on a path to being perfected. When you fully understand the cross and the power of what Jesus did, it will blow your mind.

Afterword

THE GOSPEL TRUTH

DID YOU KNOW THE WORD *GOSPEL* literally means "good news"? The Good News or the Gospel, tells us of God's plan to keep us from going to hell and being separated from Him for eternity. If we really want to understand the Good News, we have to understand all the bad stuff or the reasons why we need God and His good news.

The Bible very clearly tells us that we are ALL sinners. It is strong language but it has to be. God doesn't want to tickle your ears and protect your feelings; He wants to save your soul.

> For all have sinned and fall short of the glory of God.
> —ROMANS 3:23

We have all heard the story of Adam and Eve. As a direct result of their sin, their giving in to Satan's lies and their own temptation, every part of us now has been corrupted by sin. That is your mind, your emotions and your flesh. When Adam and Eve lived in the Garden of Eden, they walked and talked with God every day. Ever since "The Fall" we no longer seek that relationship with God.

The penalty of sin is death.

> For the wages of sin is death, but the gift of God is eternal life in Christ Jesus our Lord.
>
> —ROMANS 6:23

This scripture tells us that when you sin you earn death. It tells us that if you live in sin and continue to sin you deserve to die and spend forever separated from God. Why is being separated from God so important? When Adam and Eve lived with God they had everything they needed. They didn't know hunger, sickness, or disease. They didn't even know anger. They lived in perfect peace and abundance. When they were separated from God, that all changed.

God made it easy for them. They only had to do one thing which was to obey God and not eat the fruit of the tree of knowledge of good and evil. Satan came along as a serpent; he deceived Eve, convincing that God was holding something back from them. Even though they had everything they ever wanted, Adam and Eve chose to eat the fruit and taste evil. Because of this, they were cast out of the Garden of Eden and made to work the land. They discovered their nakedness and exposure to the curse.

So what does the Good News say?

After the fall in the garden it was impossible for man to work his way back to God so He created a plan to come to us through Jesus.

Jesus died for us all even though He never met you or me. He was beaten, whipped and then nailed to a tree on a hill until He died. He did that for you. Jesus came to show us God's love for us.

> But God demonstrates his own love
> for us in this: while we were still
> sinners, Christ Jesus died for us.
> —ROMANS 5:8

This tells us that even though we deserved to die, Jesus came to take our place. He died instead of you and me. Three days later He arose from the dead, conquering hell, death, and the grave. There was no power on earth or in hell that God couldn't overcome.

You are saved through faith in Christ.

> For it is by grace you have been saved, through faith—and this is not from ourselves, it is the gift of God—not by works, so that no one can boast.
>
> —EPHESIANS 2:8–9

No man can take the credit for you being saved, only God.

As you start to read the Bible and really dig into the Scriptures, you will learn so much about yourself. You will see how certain decisions shaped your life. But you will also learn that God has a habit of taking broken people and making them brand new.

Are you ready to make the best decision of your life? Are you ready to say, "Yes, I believe in Jesus"?

> If you declare with your mouth, "Jesus is Lord," and believe in your heart that God raised him from

the dead, you will be saved. For it
is with your heart that you believe
and are justified, and it is with your
mouth that you profess your faith
and are saved.

—ROMANS 10:9–10

We have to understand that you are not
saved by just saying words. You must mean
what you say. God sees your heart. You need
to truly repent of your sins and have faith in
Jesus.

You don't need to have all the answers.
You don't even need to own a Bible to have
salvation. Get alone, check your heart, take
a breath, and just say this prayer.

---

*Lord Jesus, for too long I've kept
You out of my life. I know that I
am a sinner and that I cannot save
myself. No longer will I close the
door when I hear You knocking. By
faith I gratefully receive Your gift
of salvation. I am ready to trust
You as my Lord and Savior. Thank
You, Lord Jesus, for coming to*

*earth. I believe You are the Son of
God who died on the cross for my
sins and rose from the dead on the
third day. Thank You for bearing
my sins and giving me the gift of
eternal life. I believe Your words
are true. Come into my heart, Lord
Jesus, and be my Savior. Amen.*

THE QUESTIONS
AND THE ANSWERS

My life experiences may seem crazy. It may
even sound like I made it all up. But I am
telling the truth.

Through writing this book and looking
back on my life, I can clearly see that the
devil had an agenda to stop me. The enemy
did everything he could to kill me, shame
me, destroy my relationships, and drive me
insane. When I said yes to God, He changed
it all around. Everything that I did wrong
and all my sin was wiped clean. I had a clean
slate. I was able to trust God to heal hurt
from all of the wrong people did to me.

From the time that I got saved, it has been such a journey. I had lots of questions for God and I wanted answers. I knew Jesus was real and I knew in my heart that Jesus would return. None of that explained why I had been through so much. Why did God let me go through all this hurt? Why did I have to bury my baby? Why have I had eleven brain surgeries, five neck surgeries, seven abdominal surgeries and so much more? If God is love, why did my own father hate me so much? Why did I stay in an abusive relationship?

Ok so first of all, I know this may be your first exposure to deliverance. I had never heard of it, I didn't know what it was until it was happening but I KNEW I needed it. Is it weird? Definitely! It's not usual to be talking about demons let alone telling them to get out of you. But let's look at that.... Why is it weird? I'm not the only one that needs this, trust me. There are A LOT of people out there battling what they think is a bad life, bad luck or bad health when really, it's spiritual. The devil has been working hard on people to make sure that we didn't know about deliverance. He doesn't want us catching on to him and getting free. He wants our souls with him for eternity in hell. Plain and straight.

In James 4:7, the Bible tells us, *"Submit yourselves, then, to God. Resist the devil and he will flee from you."* This is what I did. I said yes to God, I said yes to Jesus and I was willing to do whatever it took to get set free. Jesus has already paid the ultimate price. He died a HORRIFIC death but when he did that, he did that in place of you and me. The power behind the cross in the natural and the spirit realm is phenomenal. There are several libraries of books that discuss that. But…I said yes, ok. I resisted the devil by speaking with a qualified, anointed, appointed, deliverance minister who literally called out the devil. He commanded the devil to get out of me; leave and never return. Obviously you will understand I am really simplifying things but it is so you can understand.

The devil has been on the earth, shock horror. He isn't in hell with a pitchfork as everyone thinks. He's here, right now, doing everything he can to fill hell. He hasn't limited himself to the obvious with eight-car pile up's, devil worshippers and mass murderers.... Oh no! The enemy has much more subtle ways of affecting your life, including sicknesses and disease. When you start getting into it and getting out of it, you will be amazed, truly amazed at how blind you've been, how stupid you've been. But my goodness, how awesome Jesus is for what He did. Yes. He was the Son of God, but while He was on that cross, He was bleeding and hurting as a man. When they whipped Him so hard, you could see his internal organs. He did that as if it was you or me being whipped. Why? Because He loves you. He loves you and so does God. Jesus came to manifest God's heart on earth. He came to show an earth that was rife with stinking thinking and even worse actions, what love truly was.

> They cried out to the Lord...and he delivered them from their distress.
> —PSALM 107:6

This is a cry that comes from the heart. A heart that truly looks to God and says, look I'm sorry, I really repent, please help me get free, my God. What God says, He does. It may not always be exactly when we want it but He does it in His time. He isn't trying to hold out on you or make you suffer a bit more. He's working everything together in your life, so that it all comes at just the right time. You just have to stay in faith, stay trusting, hold on and say "God, I don't know what's going on, but I know Your Word told me I'm getting delivered and I'm holding on believing for it." If it's in the Bible, it's going to happen! Go ahead and say to Him, "God, Your word says if I cry out to You, You will deliver me, this is me crying out. Deliver me from my enemies. Show up as my Lord and Saviour." Watch and see what He will do.

Reading the Bible out loud and declaring those scriptures over your life and family is really powerful. Just by saying these out loud and feeling it with your heart, is enough to make a shift in the spirit realm. It's how you take hold of those promises. You keep saying them until the breakthrough comes and then you give God the glory. God has so many promises for us and you will find them in your Bible!

For anyone reading this that has lost a child, I can say, it was hard. I will not lie to you. But now, I know I'm getting my baby back again. I know I will see her in heaven and all of heaven will hear me scream with joy when I get her. My hurt over Layla, was healed over time with God. It was much like how if you need a lot of operations, they don't do them all at once because you couldn't handle it. This was the same. God healed, bit by bit. I won't know the answers to all of my questions about her until I get to heaven and Jesus will sit down with me and tell me but he has answered a lot. Now, instead of that gut wrenching pain in the pit of my stomach, I have such love and joy when I think about her. I love her with all of my heart. We talk about her all the time and not in sadness. She's ours and we will see her again. If you do have a child or any loved one in heaven, ask God to heal you of the pain. Ask him to set you free from the trauma. Watch and see what he will do.

I asked God to tell me why she died and He showed me things I'm keeping private. If you are on this path, ask God, He will show you. He will do whatever it takes to get you healed, after all, His son died that we might live.

As for the toxic abusive relationship, that's called a soul tie. We were not created to have more than one sexual partner and we are to be married before we have sex. Why? Well, surprise surprise: it's not because God is trying to ruin your fun. It's because there are genuine spiritual implications of it. He's trying to protect you. God created sex as a gift to enjoy between a man and a woman who are married.

> Or do you not know that he who is
> joined to a prostitute becomes one
> body with her? For, as it is written,
> "The two will become one flesh."
> —1 CORINTHIANS 6:16, ESV

Sex involves your mind, body and soul. When you have casual sex, you create a bond with them, whether you like it or not. It's similar to gluing two pieces of wood together and then ripping them apart. One piece will have bits of the other still attached. The bond has been created but once it's been separated, the two will still be longing for something or someone. They long for wholeness.

How many times have women given themselves to a man who was taking advantage of them? They thought that if they slept with him, it would make him like them. Wrong! What it does, is it makes you emotionally and spiritually connected and then when he's treating you like rubbish, guess who's going to be feeling really depressed, alone or not good enough!

But there is hope! Just repent! Ask God to forgive and He will, always. Just make sure you don't fall back into that behavior.

I would be doing you a complete disservice if I didn't address my trip to the medium. Wow! What an idiot I was. At the time, I thought I was doing what everyone else did. Sure it's harmless fun. It's not really real anyway, right? Wrong! It's very real. Yes, there are people out there pretending to be mediums just so they can get your money but there are plenty out there that are very real. Only they aren't talking to your dead loved ones, they are talking to demons pretending to be your dead loved ones. By you connecting with them, you are potentially inviting them right to you! This is what happened to me.

Let's be honest, is it really worth hearing something you already know from a stranger while you are potentially bringing home demons to wreck your life? You might be rolling your eyes or thinking, "yea right," but really... can you afford to risk it?

And while we are here, I should probably address the trend of *The Secret*. Guess what? It's not a secret. It's witchcraft. While you may enjoy some success and some power maybe even wealth as a result of following the book's teachings, good things you experience won't last long. Soon, they will come crashing down as the devil calls in that favour he's given you.

You really have to be careful with these things. Take a step back going on the understanding that mankind has been around for thousands of years and suddenly, just suddenly there is this "new" way of praying to the Universe that will suddenly help you manifest all your material hopes and dreams? Nope. That, my friend is deception.

Praying to the universe is indeed witchcraft. Just because it's been repackaged in a nice book and doesn't use the word *witchcraft* doesn't make it any less witchcraft. It is what it is. It's not some new thing—something the human race has missed out on until you came along. It's been around for a long time. It's just that someone has repackaged it, wrote a book with a pretty cover, and made a DVD and monopolized on it. And now a large part of humanity are out there practicing witchcraft without realising. But there's hope. Again, just repent, ask God to forgive you and He, will but above all things, do not start doing it again.

What we don't understand is that a lot of our needs and wants are really just our flesh, our mind, spirit and soul. When God heals and delivers you, your perception on life changes. Your heart's desires change. You see this life for what it really is and it's gone in the blink of an eye. So stop spending it on things that really don't matter and move into God's will for your life. When you are aligned with God's will for your life, that's living the purpose you were created for.

Then you will really see satisfaction, you will know JOY like you've never known it and you will have peace like you never knew existed. Does God ever give us the good stuff? Sure, He loves to bless His children. He's a good father.

I don't want to get too heavy in this but just know, there's a WHOLE world out there you knew nothing about. I'm telling you, get committed to living the life you were created for. Get ready to get rid of all the nonsense in your life and get right with God and start praying. Read your Bible and get ready to meet with God in a BIG way. IF you are willing, He is able. He loves you and He's not going to force you to have a relationship with Him, but why wouldn't you? I think it's safe to say, that if you could talk with the creator of the universe, it's a good idea to take that chance.

So we have come to the end of our journey here, I have bared all and tried to explain as much as I can. You have a lot to think on, I am sure, reading all this and I suggest you pray about it.

I have been saved almost five years now

and in that time God took me on a journey of healing me, delivering me and also showing me that I wasn't the massive screwup that I thought I was. I've shown you some of my questions and answers as I hope they may answer some of yours to help you make that important decision to accept Jesus as your Lord and Saviour. When you say YES to Jesus, you will begin a journey of wholeness. Ever since I said yes and I was open to God peeling back the layers on me, knocking down the walls I had built around my heart and revealing the truths to me, I can stand now proud of where I've been and who I've become. I can stand now and say yes I was blind but now I see. Very clearly.

I am now—finally free.

CPSIA information can be obtained
at www.ICGtesting.com
Printed in the USA
LVHW012115221120
672397LV00025B/647